FANTASTIC SCIENCE JOURNEYS

A TRIP THROUGH THE HUMAN BODY

BY CHRISTINE FIGORITO

Gareth Stevens
PUBLISHING

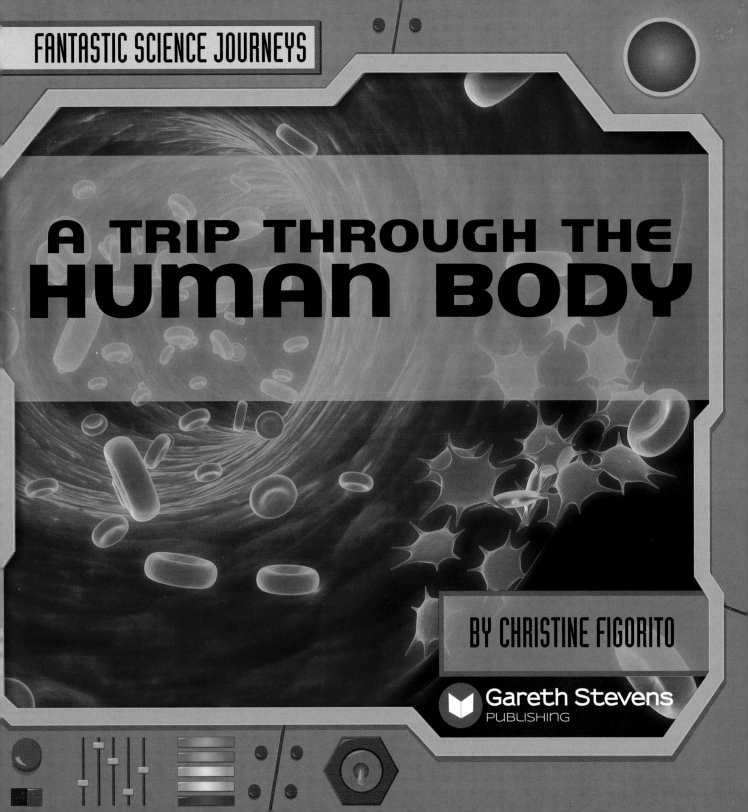

Please visit our website, www.garethstevens.com. For a free color catalog of all our high-quality books, call toll free 1-800-542-2595 or fax 1-877-542-2596.

Library of Congress Cataloging-in-Publication Data

Figorito, Christine, 1971- author.
 A trip through the human body / Christine Figorito.
     pages cm. — (Fantastic science journeys)
 Includes bibliographical references and index.
 ISBN 978-1-4824-2006-7 (pbk.)
 ISBN 978-1-4824-2005-0 (6 pack)
 ISBN 978-1-4824-2007-4 (library binding)
 1. Human body—Juvenile literature. 2. Human physiology—Juvenile literature. I. Title.
 QP37.F54 2015
 612—dc23

                                  2014029431

First Edition

Published in 2015 by
Gareth Stevens Publishing
111 East 14th Street, Suite 349
New York, NY 10003

Copyright © 2015 Gareth Stevens Publishing

Designer: Sarah Liddell
Editor: Ryan Nagelhout

Photo credits: Cover, pp. 1, 13, 15 (synapse), 19 (main), 25 Sebastian Kaulitzki/Shutterstock.com; pp. 5, 29 racorn/Shutterstock.com; pp. 7, 21 Alex Luengo/Shutterstock.com; p. 9 (main) Nerthuz/Shutterstock.com; p. 9 (brain hemispheres) decade3d/Shutterstock.com; p. 11 SPRINGER MEDIZIN/Science Photo Library/Getty Images; p. 15 (main) martynowi.cz/Shutterstock.com; pp. 17, 19 (tendons) DM7/Shutterstock.com; p. 23 Matthew Cole/Shutterstock.com; p. 27 SCIEPRO/Science Photo Library/Getty Images.

Printed in the United States of America

CPSIA compliance information: Batch #CW15GS: For further information contact Gareth Stevens, New York, New York at 1-800-542-2595.

CONTENTS

Words in the glossary appear in **bold** type the first time they are used in the text.

OUR AMAZING BODIES

Our bodies do incredible things. We run, jump, sing, and shout. At the same time our heart is beating, our lungs are helping us breathe, and our stomach is growling.

Do you wonder why our bodies do all these things? We're going to find out! Imagine you can shrink yourself until you're as small as an ant. Now, get into our special, tiny ship. It's so small it fits into an ear. We're going on a trip through the human body!

THAT'S FANTASTIC!

Our body holds about 6 quarts (5.6 liters) of blood. It goes through the body three times every minute. In one day, our blood travels a total of 12,000 miles (19,300 km)!

Our ship will take us through all the amazing parts that make up our body!

5

ANATOMY OF THE HUMAN BODY

The human body is amazing. Humans are many different shapes and sizes, but we all have the same basic body parts. The study of these parts is called anatomy.

The body is divided into systems. Each system has a very important job, and the systems work together to keep you thinking, breathing, and moving. Let's start up our ship and get ready to explore some of these systems together. Let's fire up the engines and take off!

THAT'S FANTASTIC!

Your body grows faster in the first two years of your life than at any other time. A newborn baby can't do much, but when she's two years old, she walks and talks!

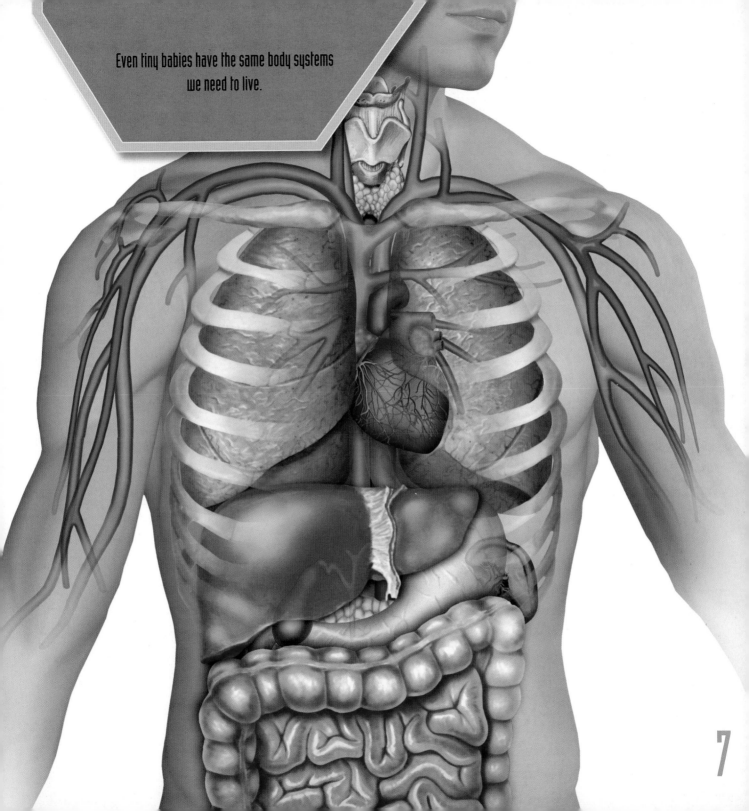

Even tiny babies have the same body systems
we need to live.

7

YOUR BODY'S COMPUTER

We're going to explore a man named Marty. He's going to let us take our ship through his body. We fly into Marty's ear, but we're so small he can't even feel it. The first thing we see is a pinkish-gray, wrinkled organ. That's his brain!

The brain works like a computer. It tells all the other parts of the body what to do. The brain is inside the skull, which is the name for the bones in the head that protect the brain from getting hurt.

THAT'S FANTASTIC!

The brain is divided into **hemispheres**. The left hemisphere controls the right side of the body, and the right hemisphere controls the left side of the body. Sounds backward, doesn't it?

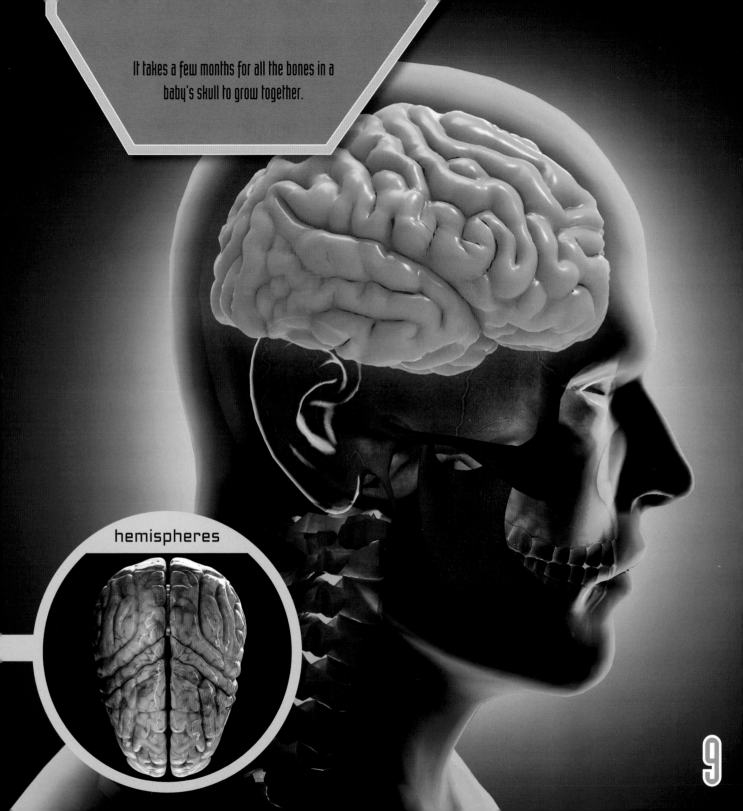

It takes a few months for all the bones in a baby's skull to grow together.

hemispheres

9

Marty's brain weighs about 3 pounds (1.4 kg), the size of most adult brains. It has three main parts. The top part, called the cerebrum, is the biggest. It has cracks and folds, and is the "thinking" part of the brain.

The cerebellum is in back, tucked under the cerebrum. It controls balance and movement. The third part, called the brain stem, is at the bottom of the brain. It controls things like breathing, heartbeat, hunger, and pain.

THAT'S FANTASTIC!

Is there such a thing as brain food? Yes! Foods like fish, walnuts, and kiwi help memory and learning. Many foods have glucose, a type of healthy sugar for your brain.

Different parts of our brain control different parts of our body.

cerebrum

brain stem

cerebellum

11

A BUNCH OF NERVES!

Marty's brain can't run his body by itself. At the back of the brain, you'll see a long bunch of **nerves** that runs down his back. This is called the spinal cord, and with the brain, it makes up the first system we see on our trip, the nervous system.

Nerves are made up of **neurons**. Neurons send messages back and forth from Marty's brain to all parts of the body. The body contains billions and billions of neurons.

THAT'S FANTASTIC!

If you touch a hot stove, neurons send a pain message from your finger to your brain. Your brain sends a message back through neurons to tell your muscles to pull that finger away!

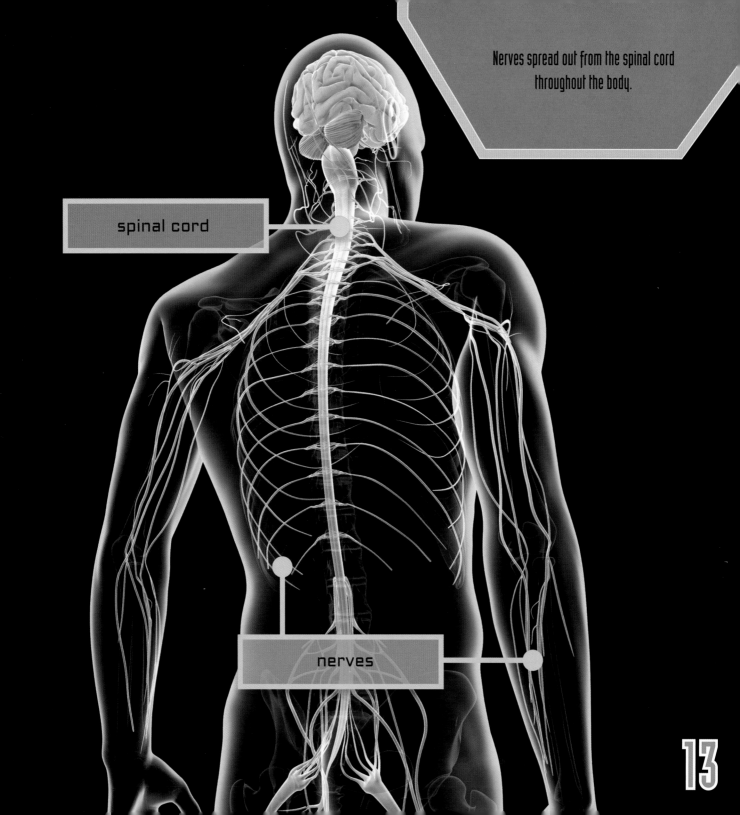

Nerves spread out from the spinal cord throughout the body.

spinal cord

nerves

13

DOWN THE SPINE

Let's follow Marty's spinal cord in our ship. Even though we can't see them, neurons are sending messages back and forth from his brain to his body at about 200 miles (320 km) per hour!

Suddenly our ship starts to move up and down. Marty's arm is moving! His eyes must have seen someone he knows, and his brain told his hand to wave hello. Neurons carry this message, but something else is making his arm move. We'll turn our ship to find out.

THAT'S FANTASTIC!

The place where a neuron connects to another neuron is called a synapse. This comes from the Greek work *synaptien*, which means "to join together."

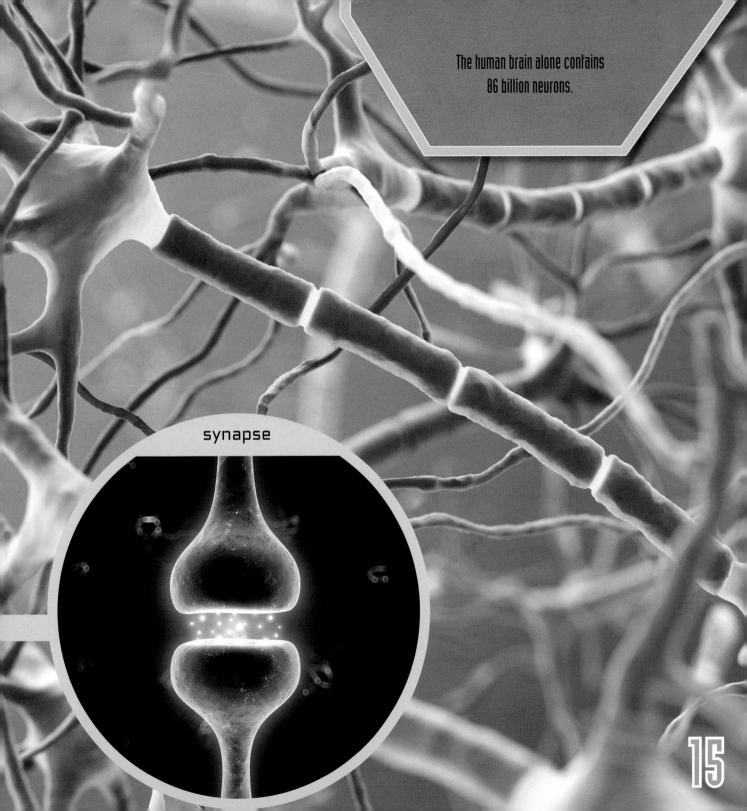

The human brain alone contains
86 billion neurons.

synapse

15

MOVE THOSE MUSCLES

Marty's arm wouldn't be able to move without muscles. Muscles give the body power. They're made up of stretching **tissue**, like the stuff that makes rubber bands. They work by tightening and relaxing.

There are three kinds of muscles. **Skeletal** muscles move the parts of the body that make us run and jump. Cardiac muscles are muscles in the heart that keep it beating. Smooth muscles move food through the body, control the blood **vessels**, and help the body go to the bathroom.

THAT'S FANTASTIC!

Skeletal muscles are voluntary, meaning we can control them. Cardiac and smooth muscles are involuntary, which means they work without us telling them what to do.

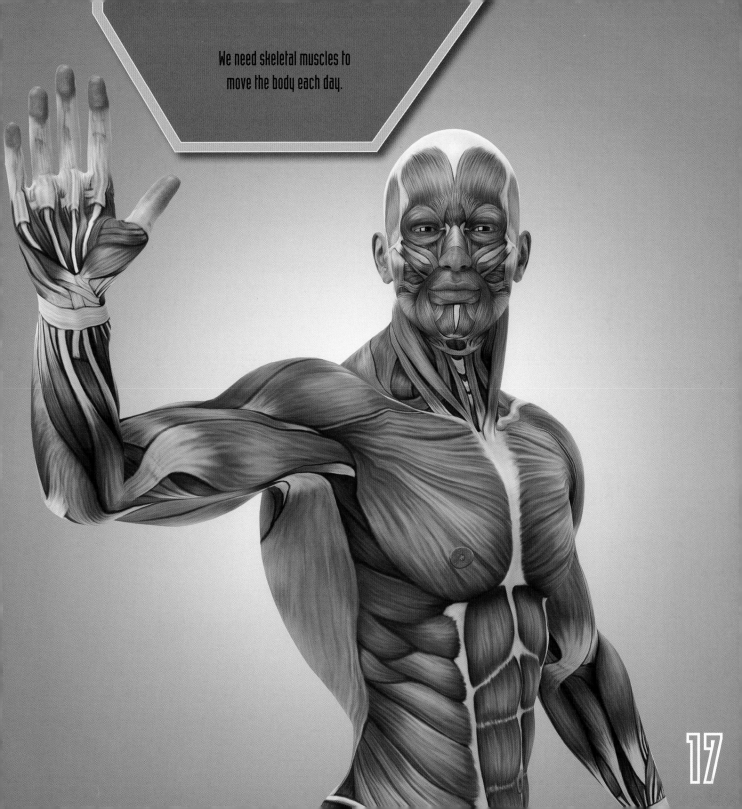

We need skeletal muscles to
move the body each day.

17

OH THEM BONES

Muscles are rubbery, so how does Marty's body stand up straight? Skeletal muscles are attached to his bones, which make up the skeletal system. We see something like ropes connecting Marty's arm muscles to his bones. These ropes are called tendons.

Marty's bones work with his muscles so he can wave. His brain sent a message through neurons to his arm muscles, which answered by moving his bones to make him wave! These bones also keep Marty's organs safe.

THAT'S FANTASTIC!

A newborn baby has around 350 bones. As people grow, some bones fuse, or grow together. By adulthood, people have 206 bones.

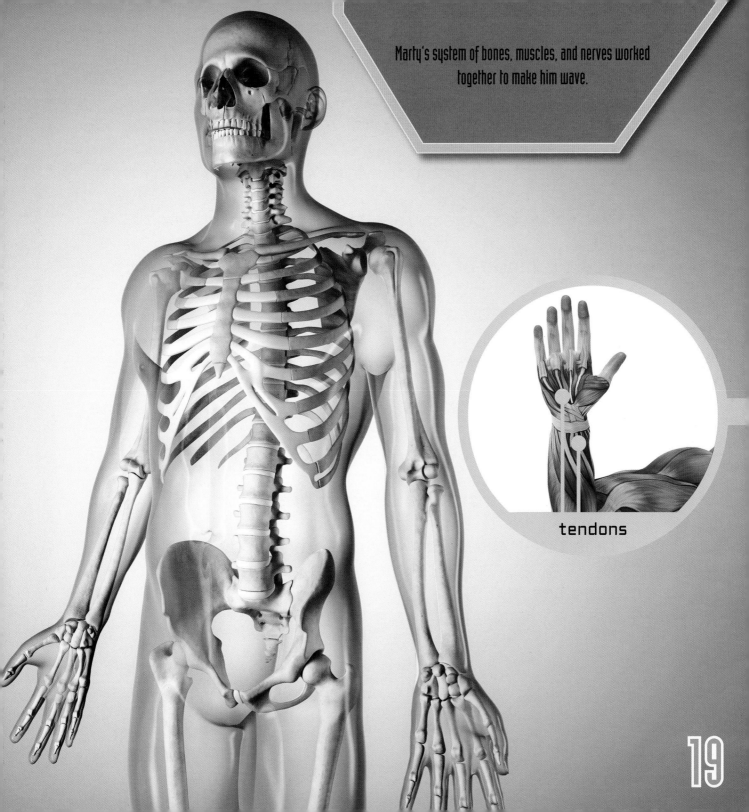

Marty's system of bones, muscles, and nerves worked together to make him wave.

tendons

19

THE HEART AND LUNGS

We take our ship to Marty's chest and see a pear-shaped object. This must be the heart! The heart is made of cardiac muscles that **pump** blood through your body.

The heart is two pumps in one. The right side gets blood from Marty's body and sends it to the lungs. The left side gets blood from the lungs and sends it back into his body. Lungs take waste gases out of Marty's blood, and the gases leave Marty's body when he breathes out.

THAT'S FANTASTIC!

Blood doesn't just slosh around Marty's body! It travels through blood vessels. They carry blood between the heart and all his body parts. This movement is called circulation.

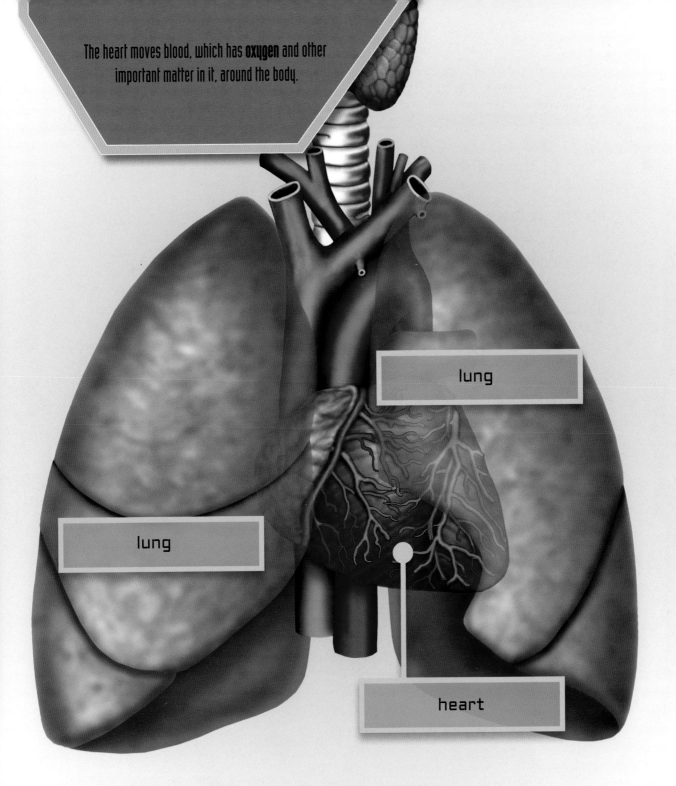

The heart moves blood, which has **oxygen** and other important matter in it, around the body.

lung

lung

heart

THE JOURNEY OF MARTY'S LUNCH

In the middle of Marty's body is a long tube that starts in his mouth. Let's follow this tube, which is called the esophagus. Marty must be eating lunch, because food is moving from his throat down to his stomach.

His stomach is a stretchy sack that looks somewhat like the letter "J." It's like a mixer, smashing food into tiny pieces. Special juices in the stomach help break down food and kill bacteria in it.

THAT'S FANTASTIC!

It might only take you a few minutes to finish a meal, but it takes your body nearly 12 hours before it has completely broken down your food.

MARTY'S BODY PARTS

esophagus

lungs

heart

liver

stomach

large intestine

small intestine

bone

muscle

Let's follow Marty's lunch as it moves through his **digestive** system. The food leaves the stomach and goes to the small **intestine**. It looks like a long tube bunched under Marty's stomach. It breaks down the food even more so his body can take in the fuel he needs to live.

The large intestine is food's last stop! It takes what's left of the food, the part the body can't use, and pushes it out as waste. It comes out when Marty goes to the bathroom.

THAT'S FANTASTIC!

The trip from Marty's mouth to his large intestine is more than 30 feet (9 m) long! His food is broken down and used to help his body stay healthy.

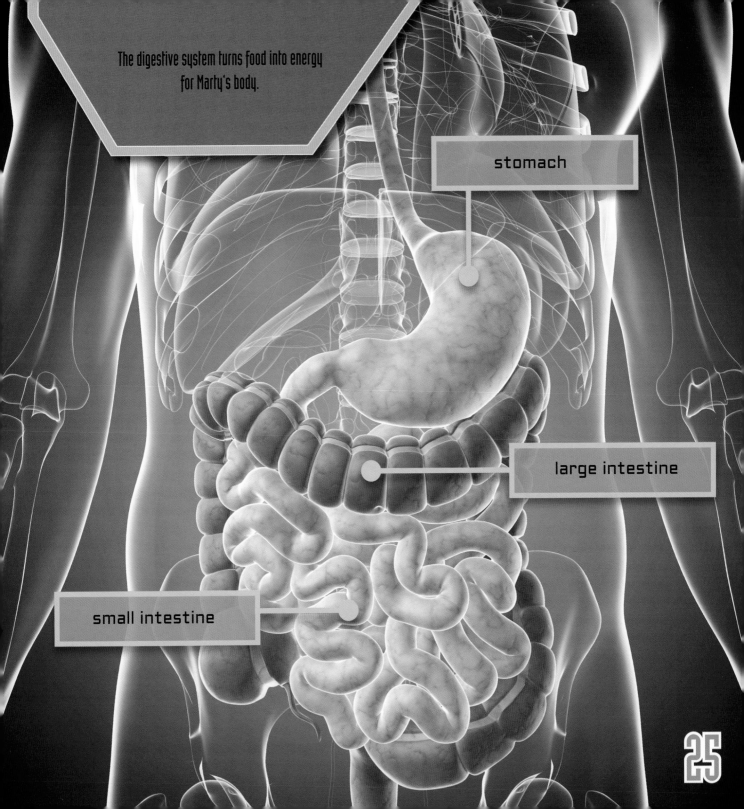

The digestive system turns food into energy for Marty's body.

stomach

large intestine

small intestine

25

CLEANING UP

Our ship also takes us to other parts of the body that collect wastes. We see the **liver** and two **kidneys**. They help clean Marty's blood. **Glands** are all over the body and make things called hormones, which are chemicals that make the body do different things.

Now it's time to leave Marty's body. Outside, we see the biggest organ of all, the skin. It covers and protects everything. Without skin, his bones, muscles, and organs would be hanging out!

THAT'S FANTASTIC!

The body has many other systems that help it stay healthy. For example, the immune system works with the blood and skin to fight disease.

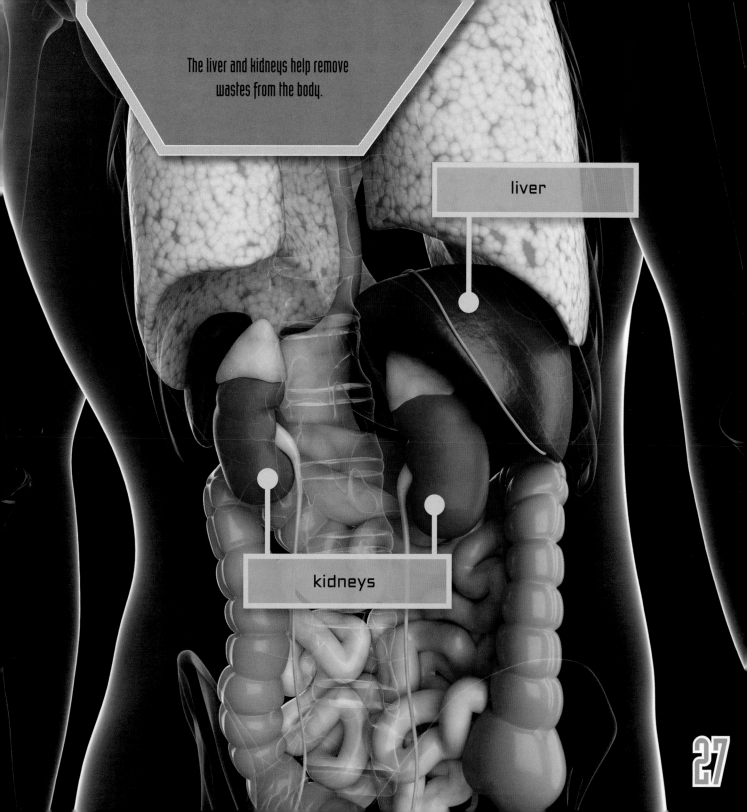

The liver and kidneys help remove wastes from the body.

liver

kidneys

KEEP IT RUNNING!

You need to keep your body in good shape! It's important to get some exercise every day. Exercise keeps you strong and full of energy. You also need to eat healthy foods to give your body the energy it needs.

Checking out Marty's insides showed us how everything works together. Your brain tells the other organs in your body how to work, but each part has an important job. Thanks for coming on our trip through this amazing machine!

THAT'S FANTASTIC!

To keep your body healthy, you should also get plenty of sleep, brush your teeth at least twice a day, and wash your hands often! Washing hands keeps away bacteria that make you sick.

Eating well and staying active are important ways you can stay healthy.

GLOSSARY

digestive: having to do with the body parts that break down food inside the body so that the body can use it

gland: an organ that releases chemical substances called hormones that tell the body what to do

hemisphere: one of the two halves of the brain

intestine: a tube where food is digested

kidney: an organ that removes waste from the blood

liver: a large organ that changes substances in blood

nerve: a thin part of the body that sends messages between the brain and other body parts

neuron: responsible for carrying the messages to and from the brain; the basic unit of the nervous system

oxygen: a gas that people breathe and need to live

pump: to move blood around the body

skeletal: having to do with the body's bones

tissue: matter that forms the parts of living things

vessel: a small tube in the body that carries blood

FOR MORE INFORMATION

BOOKS

Cohen, Robert Z. *The Stomach and Intestines in Your Body.*
New York, NY: Britannica Educational Publishing, 2015.

Jennings, Ken. *The Amazing Human Body.* New York, NY:
Little Simon, 2015.

Rose, Simon. *Muscular System.* New York, NY: AV2 by Weigl,
2015.

WEBSITES

How the Body Works
kidshealth.org/kid/htbw/htbw_main_page.html
Learn how the systems of the body work together on this site.

Human Biology
kidsbiology.com/human_biology/
Learn more amazing facts about your body on this
interactive site.

Human Body for Kids
sciencekids.co.nz/humanbody.html
Find out more about keeping your body healthy here.

INDEX